20TH CENTURY
fashion
THE
60^S

MODS & HIPPIES

20TH CENTURY FASHION – THE '60s
was produced by

David West 𝕩 Children's Books
7 Princeton Court
55 Felsham Road
London SW15 1AZ

Picture Research: Carlotta Cooper/Brooks Krikler
Research
Editor: Clare Oliver
Consultant: Helen Reynolds

First published in Great Britain in 1999 by
Heinemann Library, Halley Court, Jordan Hill,
Oxford OX2 8EJ, a division of Reed Educational and
Professional Publishing Limited.

OXFORD MELBOURNE AUCKLAND
JOHANNESBURG BLANTYRE GABORONE
IBADAN PORTSMOUTH (NH) USA CHICAGO

03 02 01
10 9 8 7 6 5 4 3

ISBN 0 431 09551 5 (HB)
ISBN 0 431 09558 2 (PB)

British Library Cataloguing in Publication Data

Powe-Temperley, Kitty
Mods and hippies (1960s). - (Fashion in the twentieth
century)
1. Fashion - History - 20th century - Juvenile
literature
2. Costume - 20th century - Juvenile literature
I. Title
391'.009046

Printed and bound in Italy.

PHOTO CREDITS:
Abbreviations: t-top, m-middle,
b-bottom, r-right, l-left
Cover tl, bm & pages 3tl, 5ml, 5bl,
5tr, 5br, 6tl, 6br, 7bl, 8l, 9l, 9tr, 10t,
10b, 10-11, 11tl, 11tr, 12mr, 12-13,
13tr, 14bl, 16bl, 19tl, 19br, 20bl,
21tr, 21br, 23r, 24tl, 24bl, 26tl, 26-
27, 28tl, 28bl, 29bl, 29bm, 29tr:
Hulton Getty; Cover ml, br & pages
4-5tl, 7br, 14r, 14-15, 15tr, 22tl,
22bm, 22-23, 24-25: Redferns;
Cover bl & page 27br: Henry
Clarke © Vogue/Condé Nast
Publications Ltd; Cover m & pages
16tl, 17br: Norman Eales © Vogue/
Condé Nast Publications Ltd; Cover
mr & pages 3mr, 20r: Justin de
Villeneuve © Vogue/Condé Nast
Publications Ltd; 6bl, 7tr, 23tl:
Pictorial Press; 8r: Frank Spooner
Pictures; 12bl: NASA; 13br, 17tl:
David Montgomery © Vogue/Condé
Nast Publications Ltd; 14tl, 18tl,
22bl: Irving Solero, Courtesy of The
Museum at the Fashion Institute of
Technology, New York; 15bl: Jean
Loup Sieff © Vogue/Condé Nast
Publications Ltd; 15br: Barry
Lategan © Vogue/Condé Nast
Publications Ltd; 16tr, 26bl: Peter
Rand © Vogue/Condé Nast
Publications Ltd; 17bl: Just Jaeckin
© Vogue/Condé Nast Publications
Ltd; 18bl, 28r: Duffy © Vogue/
Condé Nast Publications Ltd; 18-
19: Horrat © Vogue/Condé Nast
Publications Ltd; 19tr, Traeger ©
Vogue/Condé Nast Publications Ltd;
20tl, 25tr: Kobal Collection; 20-21:
Don Honeyman © Vogue/Condé
Nast Publications Ltd; 25br: Lovi ©
Vogue/Condé Nast Publications Ltd;
27mr: Corbis.

With special thanks to the Picture
Library & Syndication Department
at Vogue Magazine/ Condé Nast
Publications Ltd.

*An explanation of difficult
words can be found in the
glossary on page 30.*

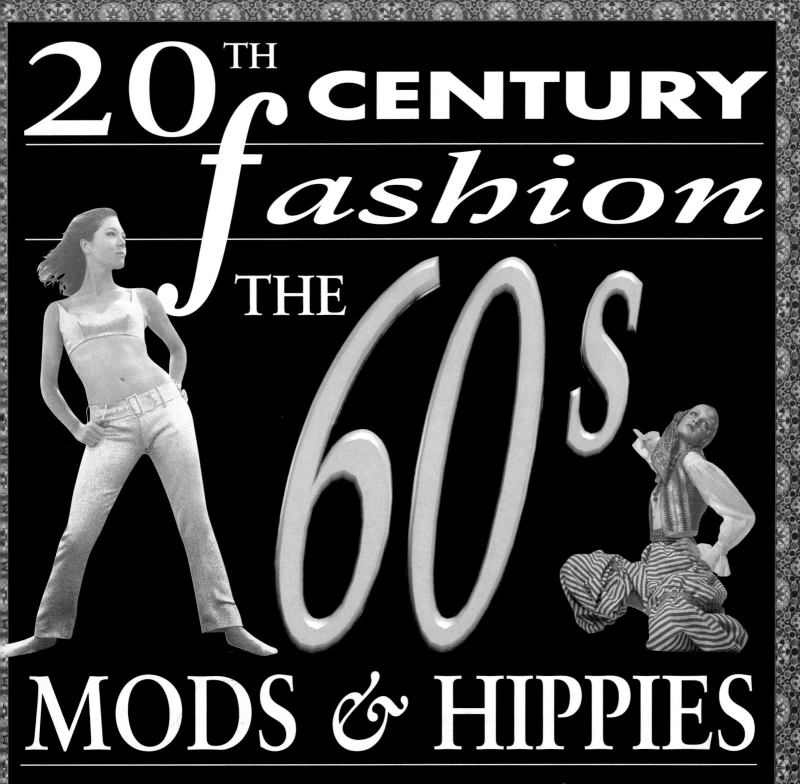

20TH CENTURY
fashion
THE 60s
MODS & HIPPIES

Kitty Powe-Temperley

Heinemann
LIBRARY

CONTENTS

THE SWINGING '60s
5

MODS & ROCKERS
6

CHANEL SUITS & PILL-BOX HATS
8

REBIRTH OF THE BOUTIQUE
10

SPAGE-AGE FASHION
12

THE MINISKIRT
14

SHOES, HATS & ACCESSORIES
16

WHEN ART BECAME FASHION
18

ICONS OF FASHION
20

DEDICATED FOLLOWERS OF FASHION
22

HIPPIE STYLES
24

EASTERN INFLUENCES
26

THE TECHNOLOGY BEHIND THE FASHIONS OF THE '60S
28

GLOSSARY
30

TIMELINE
30

INDEX
32

With greater freedom and more money in their pockets, young people set out to have a good time.

The '60s was the decade of demos. Most were non-violent, but in the Paris riots of '68, students faced armed riot police.

The SWINGING '60s

The 1960s may not have been as revolutionary as many at the time supposed, but it was a period of remarkable cultural upheaval. Attitudes towards issues of colour, class and sex changed forever.

Race riots in the United States and student-led protests against the Vietnam War throughout the West challenged the establishment. After the 1960s, relations between blacks and whites, men and women, and governments and their citizens would never be the same again.

Pop artist Andy Warhol reflected the new power of consumerism in his work.

Meanwhile, new synthetic fabrics, modern production methods and the arrival of the boutique made clothing more varied, less expensive and more accessible to young shoppers. Modern conveniences, such as TVs and cars, were at last available for large sections of society. Television in particular was responsible for the crossover between pop music and fashion.

The Pill, available from 1960, gave women sexual freedom.

In 1960, three years before the Beatles took their brand of pop music to the United States, British designer Mary Quant startled Americans by introducing new fashions aimed exclusively at the young. In the years that followed, Paris and Milan were largely ignored and 'swinging London' became the capital of the fashion world. It remained so for the rest of the decade. With the birth of the hippie movement, however, media attention shifted across the Atlantic to California. The decade ended on a hippie note: the biggest-ever youth festival in Woodstock.

A call to 'ban the bomb' was expressed in demos, and through fashion – this dress features CND peace symbols.

MODS & ROCKERS

To 'ton-up' meant to go faster than 100 mph (160 kph) on your motorbike.

While the American 'youthquake' rumbled with rockabillies, surfers and folkies, British teenagers developed their own style. Some rejected the class-based identity of the 1950s teddy boys, but still wore suits, adopting a futuristic, international and modern style: they were soon labelled the mods. Others, clad in leather jackets, continued the biking tradition of the '50s 'ton-up' boys: they were the rockers.

THE BEST POSSIBLE TASTE

The modernists, or mods, drew inspiration from the 'Cool Jazz' music of the 1950s, as performed by Miles Davis and the Modern Jazz Quartet. To be modern meant to be minimalist. For the early mods this philosophy of 'less is more' meant a specific dress code: short jackets worn with drainpipe trousers, polo shirts or turtle-neck sweaters and suede shoes or boots.

MOD STYLE REVISITED

As the mod movement grew more popular, bands such as the Who and the Small Faces became associated with mod fashion, rather than jazz bands. Mod style evolved further during one of many revivals in the '80s. As a reaction to the scruffy dress of punks, these new mods took on board the natty tailoring of their predecessors. But they developed their own musical taste. Multi-racial bands such as the Specials and Madness chose to borrow the Caribbean flavours of ska and reggae instead.

Formed in '79, the Specials wore mod suits.

Just as no rocker would be seen without his bike, the essential mod accessory was the scooter. Italian makes, such as Lambrettas and Vespas were firm favourites.

The early mod style was not a matter of who you were or where you came from, but where you were going. Good taste was paramount! While those who could afford them had bespoke (hand-tailored) suits, most mods turned to chain stores or the new boutiques.

BORN TO BE WILD

Whereas the mods were linked with jazz, rockers (a name given to them by the mods) listened to rock 'n' roll, such as Elvis and Eddie Cochran. Rocker

Pop group the Small Faces took their name from the mod slang, 'face', meaning fashion leader.

Quant-style PVC coats in op art black and white geometric designs were popular with mod girls. The hair was worn short and neat.

fashion was made up of studded leather jackets, jeans and winkle-pickers. Rockers dismissed the clean, respectable 'office dress' of the mods; the mods hated the rockers' scruffy clothes.

BRIGHTON ROCK

There were several battles between the mods and rockers, most notably in Brighton in 1964. The rockers, defeated, were never again at the forefront of fashion. But their look – and their rock 'n' roll philosophy – lived on through to the '90s, inspiring the fashions of headbangers, punks and psychobillies.

The film Quadrophenia *('79), which starred Sting and Toyah Wilcox, dramatized the bitter mod-rocker rivalry of the summer of '64.*

CHANEL suits & PILL-BOX hats

Singer Bob Dylan used his lyrics to define the politics of the generation, most notably with *The Times They Are A-Changin'*. He also described one of the classiest fashion items of the decade when he sang *Leopard Skin Pill-Box Hat*. A style item for the smart lady, the pill-box was typically worn to finish off a neat suit, such as those created by French designer Coco Chanel (1883–1971).

Coco Chanel (below) designed for comfort: she wore her own creations. The look was finished off with costume jewellery or chunky pearls, squared-toed pumps and a gilt-chained, matching bag.

COCO'S BACK!

A big name during the 1930s, Chanel had closed her Paris salon at the outbreak of World War II and not reopened until '54. Throughout the '60s, her trademark suits were worn by chic, wealthy women.

FIRST LADY OF FASHION

While Jackie Kennedy was First Lady of the United States (1961–63), her Chanel-style suits, pill-box hats and bouffant hairstyle were widely copied. Her clothes were often based on her own designs and made for her by Oleg Cassini. When her husband, President John F Kennedy, was assassinated on 23 November 1963, Jackie's tragic image was flashed around the world. She remained a fashion icon.

Jackie Kennedy and her husband, John F Kennedy.

SUITS FOR THE SMART SET

The reintroduction of her signature look, collarless cardigan-jackets worn with knee-length skirts, made Chanel the most copied designer of the early 1960s. Equally appropriate at a cocktail party or in the office, the Chanel Look became a symbol of elegance, whether copied by Oleg Cassini (*b.*1913) for Jackie Kennedy or by the home dressmaker. Indeed, Chanel-style suits are still fashionable today.

Smart suits required smart hair: here, top hairdresser Vidal Sassoon trims Mary Quant's classic '60s bob.

Mary Quant's 'Viva Viva' collection of '67 drew inspiration from the contrasting borders that finished off Chanel's suits. Quant's styles and prices made costly-looking couture elegance available to a younger market.

THE POPULAR PILL-BOX

As in earlier decades, the hat was an essential element of smart women's dress. Although Chanel had often teamed her suits with a breton hat (a French peasant hat with a rolled-up brim), the pill-box was adopted by smart ladies, particularly in the United States, after the New York fashion designer Halston (1932–90) created one in beige felt for Jackie Kennedy in 1961.

A small, oval hat with straight sides and a flat top, the pill-box was first designed in 1932 by Hollywood costumier Adrian (1903–59) for actress Greta Garbo (1905–90) to wear in the film *As You Desire Me* ('31). Often made to match the two-piece suit it accented, the pill-box was usually worn on the back of the head. Its unfussy shape suited most hairstyles, from the bouffant styles favoured by the American First Lady, to the smart new bobs introduced by top London hairdresser Vidal Sassoon (*b.*1929).

Rebirth of the BOUTIQUE

The first boutiques had opened in the 1920s. Small shops within couture houses, they sold offshoots from a couturier's line: for example, Patou sportswear, or costume jewellery by Chanel. But it was in the '60s that boutiques took off, specializing in affordable up-to-the-minute fashions for the youth market.

LONDON LADY

Mary Quant (*b.*1934) was ahead of the pack when it came to breaking the hold of traditional made-to-measure tailoring. Her Chelsea boutique, Bazaar, opened in 1955, launching what came to be known as 'the London Look'. In 1965, *Vogue* proclaimed '[Quant] blazed a trail, weathered the storm for the young designers'. Mary Quant and Bazaar challenged the British retailing system. Clothing and shopping would never be quite the same again.

A customer tries on an op art suit featuring checked jacket and striped trousers, in a Carnaby Street boutique.

The first Biba store was opened by fashion guru Barbara Hulanicki in '64. It was a souk-style treasure-trove of groovy clothes and accessories.

AN ALL-ROUND SERVICE

Boutiques offered young shoppers the fun clothes, individual attention and ease of shopping that long-established department stores and chains did not. In boutiques, young shoppers did not feel intimidated by formality or by staid, 'square' shop assistants. With young, trendy staff, hip music and artistic lighting, the boutiques made young people feel at home.

Summer '66: London's Hung On You was one of the most 'happening' boutiques in town.

SECOND TIME AROUND

Second-hand shops were an inexpensive alternative to the boutique. Here, people could ignore mainstream fashion in favour of vintage clothes, army surplus and second-hand designer originals.

Trendy second-hand store, I Was Lord Kitchener's Valet.

Shop signs featured psychedelic lettering, to reflect the goods inside.

A MEETING PLACE

Throughout the 1960s, Carnaby Street was the mecca for young, adventurous shoppers in search of swinging London style, while in the United States, San Francisco became the hippie capital. Whether the fashion trend was psychedelic, ethnic or flower power, boutiques sold the gear: regimental jackets in pastel shades or bold colours, flamboyant bell-bottoms, barely-there miniskirts and tie-dyed tee shirts. Many sold accessories too, from space-age plastic rings to strings of ethnic beads. Shops such as Mr Fish, I Was Lord Kitchener's Valet, and Granny Takes a Trip promised not only to provide the merchandise, but to give shoppers a good time while they were looking for it!

SPACE-AGE *fashion*

By 1964, with the space race in full swing, some designers looked to the future for inspiration. Space-age clothes featured geometric, sculpted shapes. Most of all, they exploited the very latest materials – synthetics such as PVC, hard plastics, silver Lurex and even metallic paper.

ONE SMALL STEP FOR ... SCI-FI

In 1961, Russian cosmonaut Yuri Gagarin (1934–68) made history as the first man in space. Suddenly, space exploration was achievable, but no one knew what might be found. There was an explosion of space-based science-fiction comics, TV shows, such as *Star Trek* ('66), and films. Most concentrated on encounters with aliens. These aliens offered endless ideas for alternative ways of living – and dressing.

Space-age models pose in silver minidresses and moon boots, Paris, '69.

MAN ON THE MOON
The 1960s began with a Russian in space and ended with an American on the Moon. On 19 July 1969, the Lunar Module from the spacecraft *Apollo 11* landed Neil Armstrong and Edwin Aldrin there.

Aldrin leaves the Lunar Module to take his first steps on the Moon.

ONE GIANT LEAP FOR ... FASHION

In 1964, André Courrèges (*b*.1923) presented 'Space Age' and captured the spirit of the day. The collection included plastic goggles and astronaut helmets, silver moon boots and glitzy catsuits. Synthetic textiles gave his clothes a sculpted look, and his designs were seen as 'outrageously outer-planetary'. His coats, suits and dresses all had the same profile: rounded shoulders and stand-up collars.

With the launch of Concorde, in '67, supersonic flight would soon be available – to non-astronauts! Braniff International airline saw the connection, and sent their stewardess to the launch in space-age gear.

Cecil Gee's 'Gee-Man' outfit ('67) was designed with the man-about-space in mind! But most men chose more down-to-Earth styles as everyday attire.

TO BOLDLY GO

Pierre Cardin (*b.*1922) also showed a 'Space Age' collection in 1964. His fabrics were stark white with clear, silver or black details. Outfits included tubular or A-line jackets worn with slim trousers and short boots; minis were worn with mid-calf, knee-high or thigh-high boots. This was clothing meant for the adventurous.

In '66, Paco Rabanne took the new materials to extremes, wiring together plastic or metal tiles to make chain mail.

A METEORIC IMPACT?

Few designers explored futuristic styling for menswear. Cardin went furthest, adding zips and pockets to leather or vinyl tunics. These were to be worn over trousers tucked into moon boots, but only the ultra fashion-conscious wore them. On the high street, Cecil Gee's shiny silver 'Gee Man' outfit was more of a publicity stunt than a serious attempt to change the face of menswear! For most women, too, space-age fashions were far too outrageous. Paco Rabanne (*b.*1934) was famous for his wild creations in materials including plastic, paper and metals. But space-age styles soon modified into a more wearable form – Cardin's slim-cut trousers, for example, went on to become a fashion staple.

The MINIskirt

The miniskirt, at its debut in the mid-1960s, caused a sensation. Hemlines had been creeping up since the early '60s, but the new designs showed more leg than ever before.

Baby Doll by Courrèges, who claimed to have invented the mini.

SCHOOLGIRL CHIC

Fashion designer Mary Quant is credited with introducing the miniskirt. Following on from her successful Ginger Group designs, which featured cheap separates, Quant continued to design clothing that answered the growing need among teenagers and young adults to freely express themselves.

Like Chanel, Quant designed clothes that she would look good in. Her clothes looked best on women who had a slim, schoolgirl figure like her own. Her long-waisted pinafore dresses with their hip-level belts and pleated or flared skirts stopped just above the knee but looked much shorter than they actually were.

FUTURISTIC STYLES

But Quant was not the only designer raising hemlines. In the early 1960s, André Courrèges had shown very short skirts worn over tight-fitting trousers.

The 'Breakaway Girl' collection of '66 featured shorter-than-short Nylon minidresses, with pink paisley-print sleeves and tights.

Thigh-high minidresses in sheer fabrics brought the baby-doll look from the bedroom to the street.

The mini car was a '60s classic, shown right with customized psychedelia.

FREE LOVE
The Pill enabled women to experiment with sex before marriage without the risk of pregnancy for the first time . Later, this developed into the hippie idea of 'free love'.

The miniskirt reflected women's new freedom (left).

By '65 women were generally wearing the skirts with mid-calf boots. Courrèges' designs, with their futuristic and sharp, angular lines, were well suited to the shorter skirt lengths and made fashion headlines on both sides of the Atlantic.

A-HEM!
By 1967 miniskirts had risen from just above the knee to mid-thigh length, and were widely worn by younger women. As the decade drew to a close, designers introduced a variety of skirt lengths: a very skimpy mini, which barely covered the behind; the calf-length midi-skirt which was usually A-line in shape and was worn by women of all ages; and the maxi-length coat or skirt, which reached the ankle or the floor.

In the following decades women have continued to experiment with skirt lengths, in some instances following the lead of a designer, but generally choosing the one which most suits their own personal taste and lifestyle.

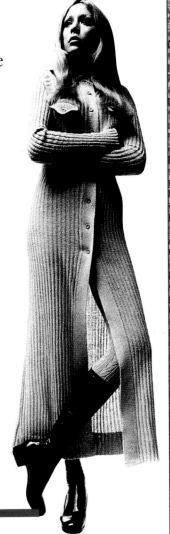

The A-line midi-skirt was a welcome fashion for women who did not feel comfortable revealing so much leg.

The maxi-length coat was often worn over the top of a minidress. Knee-high boots completed the look.

SHOES, HATS & accessories

Synthetics such as Corfam provided an easy-care alternative to suede.

Toes were squarer than in the '50s. Shoes were two-tone or hole-punched to create interesting patterns.

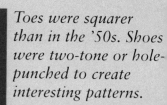

As skirts shortened, the increasing expanse of leg on view drew attention to the extremities. Shoes became more chiselled, with less heel. Flat shoes were the perfect foil to Mary Quant's textured, patterned tights.

BEAUTIFUL BOOTS

The 1960s was the decade of the boot, which was no longer treated as an item only to be worn in bad weather. In lengths from the ankle to the thigh, boots were popular with all age groups. André Courrèges' calf-length shiny white boots with clear, cut-out tops conformed to the silhouette of his space-age clothing. The leather or vinyl knee-length boot, sometimes called the go-go boot, zipped or laced up to fit the leg snugly. It remains popular today for both casual and smart dressing.

For men, ankle-length Chelsea or Beatle Boots with stacked heels and pointed winkle-picker toes were the definitive look of the early '60s, giving way mid-decade to the space boot, which, along with the cowboy boot, remained essential casualwear well into the 1970s.

This kid leather balaclava appeared in '63. Such wacky wear was warm and ultra modern.

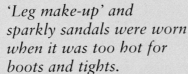

SUMMERTIME SHOES

Hippies, when not going bare foot, were most likely to be wearing simple 'Jesus' sandals with two buckled straps. For the style-conscious, strappy, jewel-encrusted sandals looked good with everything and were a breezy alternative to the boot. After 1967 styles began to appear with higher heels and thicker soles, heralding the platform shoe.

HAT TRICKS

The bobs and urchin cuts of the early 1960s were worn with an elegant pill-box or a '20s-style cloche, but more often the head was left bare. Hippies and psychedelics popularised a huge range of headgear – as well as the famous headbands, they wore huge floppy sunhats, pointed 'wizard' hats, berets, decadent top hats and peaked caps. As ever, anything went!

It was fashionable to mix patterns, shapes and textures. A crocheted cloche might be worn with plastic sunglasses, hole-punched gloves and a two-tone bag.

LASHINGS OF STYLE

The dolly-bird look drew attention to the eyes. Coats of mascara achieved the wide-eyed stare until, in '64, false lashes came on to the market. At first, each eyelash had to be stuck on individually, but soon 'falsies' came as stick-on strips. Black remained the colour of choice, but the most outrageous came in golds, silvers or coloured glitters.

Falsies were not designed to look natural!

When <u>Art</u> became fashion

Andy Warhol's pop-art 'soup' paintings soon found their way from the art gallery to the cat-walk.

In the 1960s, the boundaries blurred between art and fashion. Artists such as Bulgarian-born Christo (*b*.1935) and American Mimi Smith created clothes as works of art, while designers raided pop art and op art for patterns. On canvas or on fabric, the clever use of shapes such as circles, squares and spirals gave the illusion of movement.

JUST AN ILLUSION

Op art (or 'optical art') became a huge fashion trend. English artist Bridget Riley (*b*.1931) was a noted figure in the movement. Her black-and-white circles, zigzags, squares and rectangles were cleverly repeated to create a 3-D effect: her work seemed to recede, project out or ripple.

DIY op art: Vogue provided the pattern for this shorts suit. The fabric's strong zigzags seemed to wobble and shift as the wearer walked along.

Cecil Gee's spring collection for '66 saw men modelling op art style black-and-white leather jackets.

The illusion worked by confusing the optic nerve in the eye. Textile designers jumped at the chance to use the same trick in their fabrics. In doing so, designers such as London-based Ossie Clark (1942–96) and Paris-based Yves Saint Laurent (*b*.1936) created fashions that dazzled.

FAKING IT

Trompe l'oeil, a term that means 'to fool the eye', was another method used to create a 3-D effect. Translated into fashion, it was used to knit pretend collars or cuffs into the design of a sweater, or to give dresses contrasting belts and pockets.

HOMEMADE ART

Tie-dyeing became popular for those who preferred to make their own art. This simple technique enabled even the least artistic to create endless swirling patterns in a whole rainbow of colours. As with most fashion, streetstyle found its way off the street: tie-dyed tee shirts, shirts and dresses still sell nearly 40 years on. But tie-dye remains a hallmark of the 1960s: ask people what they wore then and the likely answer will be 'tie-dyed shirts and jeans'.

Mondrian's paintings were an inspiration as can be seen in this striking cocktail dress of '65.

Some textiles featured built-in illusions, such as moiré-effect velvet (bottom left) that shimmered and swirled in the light.

ABSTRACT ART

In '65 Saint Laurent based a collection on the work of Dutch artist Piet Mondrian (1872– 1944), who had used primary colours, along with white, grey and black, to create his geometric forms – ideal for Saint Laurent's boxy dresses.

Saint Laurent (centre) with two models.

ICONS *of fashion*

The link between media, music and fashion was central to popular culture in the 1960s. The Bond films, and TV shows such as *The Avengers* and *The Man from UNCLE,* provided role models for both sexes. Magazines such as *Mirabelle, Boyfriend* and *Fabulous,* aimed primarily at girls, featured rock and film star pin-ups, alongside tips on make-up and fashion.

The Bond movies were firm favourites at the box office, promising thrills, adventure and the latest skimpy fashions.

Twiggy's huge eyes and pouty mouth typified the '60s look: sexy, but sweet.

GIRLISH SUPERMODELS

The two most famous models of the decade were Jean Shrimpton and Twiggy. 'The Shrimp' was 17 when she began modelling; Twiggy (real name Lesley Hornby) was just 16 when she was dubbed 'the face of '66.' Twiggy had all the necessary features: a boyish figure made her the ideal clothes-horse, whether she was modelling simple minis or flowing hippie-wear. And her striking features matched the new taste for wide-eyed innocence.

Model Patti Boyd broke millions of hearts by marrying pop pin-up George Harrison.

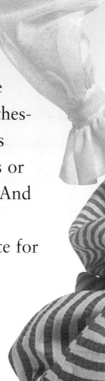

AVENGING ANGELS

Television heroines such as Cathy Gale (played by Honor Blackman) and Emma Peel (Diana Rigg) of *The Avengers* were sexy, sophisticated and strong. They dressed in skin-tight black leather or gleaming PVC catsuits.

Model Jean Shrimpton poses alongside examples of that other style classic of the decade: the mini car!

WOMEN'S LIBBERS

It was no accident that the media were portraying stronger women. The introduction of the Pill and the legalization of abortion went some way to freeing women from their traditional domestic roles. But throughout the decade feminists had to fight hard for their rights. Tired of being considered 'baby machines', these women wanted more say and more pay.

Marches kept the issues of sexual politics alive.

ONE FOR THE BOYS

The media was busy defining roles for men, too. The film, television, and particularly pop music, worlds overloaded young men with information of how they should look.

Rigg may have worn trousers as Peel in The Avengers, *but she remained the sidekick of the male lead role, Steed.*

Worse still, such information was available to young women: they could compare how their male friends' fashion sense measured up against the sex appeal of Mick Jagger, or the sleek sophistication of celluloid heroes such as James Bond!

Thus, young men as well as young women were looking carefully at their image as they found themselves challenged by their peers, and by the media, to conform to each trend as it arose.

DEDICATED
followers of fashion

The mods had paved the way for a change in attitude to menswear. For the first time since the 1700s, it was alright for men to be dandies and make an effort with their dress. Mens' fashion shifted from the conservative, classic look of the tailored suit to 'anything goes'. From the Beatle jacket in 1963, to the Carnaby Street splendour of psychedelic clothes in the mid-'60s and the effeminate styles that closed the decade, a revolution occurred in menswear.

Mick Jagger, the peacock of pop, struts his stuff in a full-sleeved shirt.

PAISLEY POWER
In the 1800s, the Scottish town of Paisley produced patterned shawls in imitation of real cashmeres. Inspired by the Mughal art of India, it was not surprising paisley covered everything in the '60s.

Men's paisley suits were not unusual.

MODS À LA MODE
Thanks to the mods' minimalist look, young men's fashions became more of an expression of individuality. The drab, three-button suit worn by men since the turn of the century was too 'establishment': style-seeking men wanted more choice!

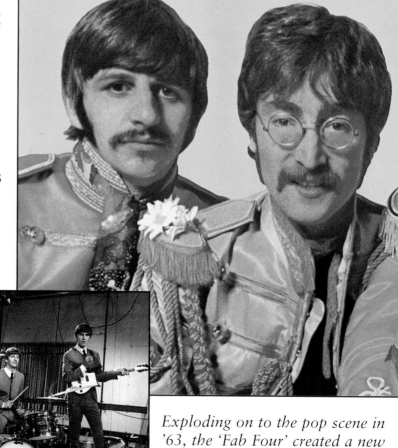

Exploding on to the pop scene in '63, the 'Fab Four' created a new fashion craze for copycat Beatle jackets and tight-fitting trousers.

From their heads to their toes, hip young men created their own 'thrown-together' style.

1967: even the men who were lost without a suit grew more dapper as the decade wore on.

BOUTIQUES FOR BOYS

Of course, men had more spending power too. They no longer needed to buy a wardrobe to 'last a lifetime'. Department stores began to offer affordable clothing in a range of styles, while new boutiques, such as His Shop and Vince, provided trendy clothing and accessories.

LIKE A RAINBOW

Ending the drab and conformist attitudes left over from World War II, coloured suits and shirts appeared in London's West End shops. White, pink, cinnamon and mustard were favourites. The desire to dress to express one's personality led to increasingly flamboyant styles. Men escaped their traditional roles in frilled dress-shirts, rainbow-coloured velvet jeans, hip-hugging trousers and ethnic, unisex kaftans.

By '67, *when they launched* Sgt Pepper, *the Beatles had embraced psychedelia in their Indian-inspired music and their decadent clothes.*

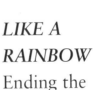

HIPPIE *styles*

The hippie look, one of the many anti-fashion statements of the 20th century, defined the 1960s. Hippie slogans such as 'Peace' and 'Love' reflected the desire to find an alternative way of living, where an individual could drop out of society to focus on the spiritual life, instead of being a slave to money.

Peaceful protest was the method chosen by most youngsters who wanted to make their views known.

BEFORE THE HIPPIES

Blossoming in 1965 in the Haight-Ashbury area of San Francisco, the hippie movement developed from the ideas of people from anti-establishment lifestyles that had gone before. Their carefree vibe came from the beats, their hedonism from the surfers, their political conscience from the folkies, and their 'turn on, drop out' attitude from the drug-using psychedelics.

By '67, the Beatles were promoting the hippie look – and its spiritual quest. They made a pilgrimage to India and had their own guru, Maharishi Mahesh Yogi (right).

Flower power was about going back to nature. The flower was a symbol of natural beauty.

Hell's Angels seemed the exact opposite of the peace-loving hippies. But these hard bikers even attended Woodstock – as bouncers!

HIPPIE CHIC

Long hair, beads, bare feet (or sandals) and bell-bottoms are what most people associate with hippie fashion, but just about anything was worn so long as it was loose-fitting and ethnic. Women wore inexpensive and colourful Indian or African cottons that were made into long skirts, shawls and 'peasant' blouses. The men teamed Eastern-style tunics with embroidered waistcoats, denim jeans or velvet trousers.

TRIPPY CLOTHES

Nicknamed the 'Summer of Love', 1967 was the height of the hippie era and saw a non-ethnic version of the clothes: in man-made fibres with psychedelic, drug-inspired patterns that complemented the music of the day.

PSYCHEDELIC PAINT
Reacting against drab conformity, hippies used body paint to adorn themselves with psychedelic motifs and flowers. The wilder your designs, the groovier you appeared.

Body paint recreated the 'way-out' hallucinations seen on an LSD 'trip.'

EASTERN influences

As the hippies turned to the East for inspiration, so did the fashion designers. At first, the hippies' mix-and-match approach to ethnic styles seemed a way to reject Western consumerism. Soon, of course, those back-to-basics kaftans were a booming business.

Egyptian make-up was teamed with a 'samurai' haircut.

HIPPIE SHAKE-UP

Disdainful of conformity, the hippie movement of the late 1960s blended the ethnic with the exotic. The world was their supermarket, especially the East. Kaftans, loosely cut ankle-length garments based on African and Arabic tribal wear, were unisex. Fibres had to be natural, so kaftans came in cotton, wool or silk. For a more tailored look, baggy Arabian pants fitted the bill. Voluminous, brightly-coloured silks and cottons made up these flamboyant, sultan-style trousers.

BOYS WILL BE GIRLS

At first, ethnic clothes were bought from small boutiques or by mail order from the mushrooming textile import businesses. Before long, streetwise fashion designers such as Ossie Clark were recreating the hippie look for themselves.

Menswear, '67-style: this braid-trimmed woollen kaftan was designed by Adolpho de Velasco.

In '67 London hosted the first hippie fashion show. Designer Michael Rainey modelled his Arabian cloak, or djellaba. Eija wore a baggy pantaloon suit by Ossie Clark.

By the end of the decade, the kaftan had even made it on to the cat-walks of haute couture houses. Wealthy women attended elegant dinners in hand-embroidered kaftans of flowing silk.

COMPLETING THE OUTFIT

Exotic accessories included raw-silk scarves in Indian prints, hand-embroidered waistcoats and beads – lots of them! Beads came in polished semi-precious stones or carved wood and were worn in long strings about the neck by both men and women.

BUILT FOR COMFORT

Eastern styles met the desire for a more 'spiritual' way of living and dressing and became the first truly unisex fashions. More practically, these loose, flowing clothes were extremely comfortable. Designed for wear in countries that could get unbearably hot, there were no tight waistbands; sleeves were loose and did not cut into the armpit. They could be worn by people of any shape or size. Fashion models remained strikingly thin, but a floor-length kaftan could cover even the most unfashionably-shaped bodies.

Photographers headed East in search of exotic backdrops. Here, a model poses in the Taurus Mountains, Turkey.

EASTERN SPIRITUALITY

Many hippies adopted chanting, vegetarianism and communal living from the ancient religions of India. The Hare Krishnas went further. In '66, the International Society for Krishna Consciousness was founded in the United States. Living in communes, members gave up meat, alcohol and sex. Followers took to the streets to convert people to their way of life.

Hare Krishnas shave their heads and wear flowing Hindu robes.

The TECHNOLOGY *behind*

In the 1960s, more than ever before, fashion proclaimed individuality, function and fun. This was made possible by the development of exciting new synthetic fabrics and by finding new ways to use existing materials such as rayon, nylon and polyester.

Designed in '66, this trousersuit came in state-of-the-art PVC.

FUELLING FASHION

Du Pont had introduced nylon, the first of many synthetic fabrics, in 1938. Under the brand names of Terylene and Crimplene, it was widely used in both underwear and outerwear because it was tough and hardwearing and took coloured dyes well.

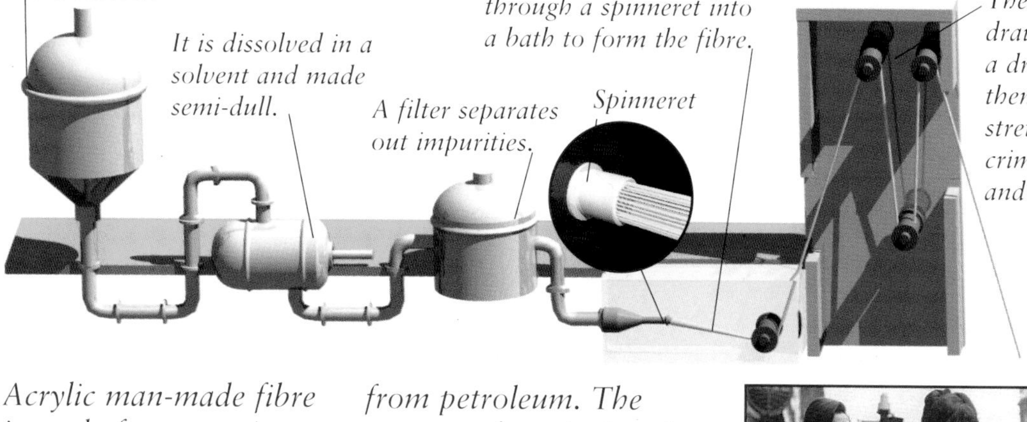

'Radical' Terylene suit ('67), by Schwartzman of Sweden.

Acrylonitrile is polymerized in the reactor.

It is dissolved in a solvent and made semi-dull.

The liquid is forced through a spinneret into a bath to form the fibre.

A filter separates out impurities.

Spinneret

The fibre is drawn through a dryer and then on to the stretcher, crimper and baler.

Acrylic man-made fibre is made from a resin chemically produced from petroleum. The process of producing the fibre is shown above.

SYNTHETIC STOCKINGS

Mary Quant, one of the first dress designers to design hosiery, capitalized on the availability of nylon in very fine deniers. In '65, she made the first patterned stockings with floral sprigs, and in '67 she followed these with nylon tights bearing her daisy logo.

Sparkling Lurex lamé was used to create space-age styles, such as these shorts and knickerbockers.

the fashions of the '60s

PRETTY POLLY

First used in furnishings, polyester was crease-resistant, quick-drying and kept its shape. It became one of the most widely used man-made fibres. Polyester and its derivative, acrylic, under the trade-names Dacron and Orlon (for outerwear) and Lycra and Antron (for underwear and swimwear), were also popular with designers.

THROW-AWAY FASHION

Fashions in materials such as paper and plastics enjoyed a brief popularity during the mid-1960s. PVC (polyvinyl chloride) was a fashionable alternative to leather.

Designer Daniel Hechter created these disposable dresses in '66.

Right is an example of a glittering metal minidress by Paco Rabanne. Below is Rabanne at work. Using aluminium, hole-punched to dramatic effect, he updated medieval chain mail into womenswear.

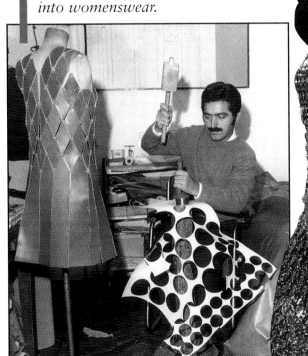

PVC dyed well and suited looks ranging from mod to space-age. Paper, reinforced with nylon, was briefly used in suits and underwear, but disposable clothes never became more than a passing trend.

FEET FIRST

Corfam, another Du Pont product, was developed as a leather substitute. It was soft and supple, and like leather, allowed feet to breathe. It was widely used for boots, especially following Mary Quant's use of it in her ankle boots.

Synthetic textiles had a huge impact on 1960s fashions, making them more colourful, more varied, and most importantly, affordable.

GLOSSARY

A-LINE Clothing that is narrow at the top and wide at the bottom.

BEATS Youth movement of the 1950s. Beats listened to modern jazz and wore workwear.

BELL-BOTTOMS Trousers that flare out at the bottom.

CASHMERE Soft wool, from the fleece of the Kashmir goat.

CLOCHE A close-fitting hat, first popular in the 1920s.

CONSUMERISM Social system based on buying and selling goods.

COUTURIER A fashion designer who makes clothes to measure.

DANDY A man who pays great attention to his clothes.

DENIER Measures the fineness of silk, rayon or nylon yarn.

DISPOSABLE CLOTHES Clothes made to be worn once or twice and then thrown away.

DOLLY BIRD A woman who looks very young and attractive.

FOLKIES Youth movement of the 1950s. Folkies listened to folk music and wore rustic clothes.

HAUTE COUTURE Expensive, made-to-measure fashions.

HEDONISM Living for pleasure.

KAFTAN Loosely-cut, ankle-length garment based on African and Arabic tribal wear.

MAXI-SKIRT An ankle- or floor-length skirt.

MIDI-SKIRT A calf-length skirt.

MINISKIRT A skirt that ends above the knee.

OP ART Art that creates an optical illusion.

PILL-BOX HAT A small, oval hat with straight sides and a flat top.

PSYCHEDELIA Visual or sound effects inspired by a mind-bending drug, such as LSD.

PVC Short for 'polyvinyl chloride'. A shiny vinyl plastic.

TIE-DYE A dyeing technique of knotting fabric so the dye makes a swirling pattern.

UNISEX Designed to be worn by men or women.

WINKLE-PICKER Shoe or boot with long, pointed toes.

FASHION HIGHLIGHT

- •Mary Quant launches in US •Valentino's first show

1

- •Courrèges opens •Jackie Kennedy appoints Oleg Cassini her official designer

1

- •Hardy Amies: menswear •Daniel Hechter opens

1

- • Mary Quant starts 'Ginger Group' •Sassoon: 'Nancy Kwan' bob

1

- •Rudi Gernreich: topless bathing suit •Courrèges: 'Space Age' •Biba opens

1

- •Yves Saint Laurent: 'Mondrian' dress •Rabanne: plastic dress

1

- •Yves Saint Laurent: ready-to-wear •Jean Muir opens •Rabanne: 'body jewellery'

1

- •Oscar de la Renta: 'Gypsy' collection •Yves Saint Laurent: knickerbocker suit

1

- •Zandra Rhodes opens •Sonia Rykiel opens •Hechter: duffle coats

1

- •Rei Kawakubo founds Comme des Garçons •The Gap founded

1

TIMELINE

	WORLD EVENTS	TECHNOLOGY	FAMOUS PEOPLE	ART & MEDIA
0	•Belgian Congo granted independence	•Laser invented •US nuclear submarine Triton circumnavigates the world underwater	•Leonid Brezhnev President of USSR •Madonna born	•Yves Klein: Anthropométries •Alfred Hitchcock: Pyscho
1	•Bay of Pigs invasion of Cuba •Berlin Wall built •OPEC formed	•Yuri Gagarin is the first man in space •Renault 4 first produced	•Ernest Hemingway commits suicide •Ballet star Nureyev defects from USSR	•Claes Oldenburg opens 'The Store', selling plastic replicas of food
2	•Cuban missile crisis •Algeria independent from France	•Telstar satellite launched •Silicon breast implant	•Death of Marilyn Monroe •Georges Pompidou is French PM	•Warhol: One Hundred Campbell's Soup Cans •Burgess: A Clockwork Orange
3	•Nuclear Test Ban Treaty signed by USSR, UK & USA	•Philips introduce audio cassette tapes •Valium introduced in US	•Assassination of John F Kennedy •Bruce Reynolds leads Great Train Robbery	•Roy Lichtenstein: Wham! •Beach Boys: Surfin' USA
4	•UN sanctions against S Africa •Vietnam War begins •PLO formed	•Word processor invented •Moog synthesizer invented	•Muhammad Ali world heavyweight champion •Mandela jailed in S Africa	•The Hollies: In the Hollies Style •Goldfinger •A Fistful of Dollars
5	•India & Pakistan at war •End of capital punishment in UK	•Completion of France–Italy road tunnel through Mt Blanc	•Assassination of Malcolm X	•Bridget Riley: Arrest I •Doctor Zhivago •The Sound of Music
6	•Cultural revolution in China	•Fuel injection introduced for car engines in UK	•England football team win World Cup	•David Hemmings: Blow-Up •Bob Dylan: Blonde on Blonde
7	•Six-Day War between Arabs & Israelis	•First heart transplant •Dolby invents noise reduction system for stereos	•Che Guevara killed in Bolivia •Artists Gilbert & George first meet	•Disney: Jungle Book •Beatles: Sgt Pepper's Lonely Hearts Club Band •The Doors: The Doors
8	•USSR invades Czechoslovakia •Student riots in Paris •Tet Offensive, Vietnam	•Aswan Dam completed	•Assassination of Martin Luther King Jr •Yuri Gagarin dies in plane crash	•Chitty Chitty Bang Bang •2001: A Space Odyssey •Marvin Gaye: I Heard it through the Grapevine
9	•Stonewall Uprising: beginning of Gay Rights movement	•Neil Armstrong takes first moon walk •Concorde's maiden flight	•Marriage of John Lennon & Yoko Ono •Ronald & Reggie Kray jailed	•Woodstock music festival, USA

INDEX

acrylic 29
Adrian 9
A-line 13, 14, 15, 30
Amies, Hardy 30
Apollo 11, 12
Armstrong, Neil 12, 31
army surplus 11
Avengers 20, 21

Beatles 5, 22, 23, 24, 31
Beatle boot 16
Beatle jacket 22
beats 24, 30
bell-bottoms 11, 25, 30
Biba 10, 30
body paint 25
Bond, James 20, 21, 31
boot 6, 12, 13, 15, 16, 17, 21, 29
boutique 5, 7, 10, 11, 23, 26
breton hat 9

Cardin, Pierre 13
Carnaby Street 10, 11, 22
cashmere 22, 30
Cassini, Oleg 8, 9, 30
catsuit 12, 21
Chanel, Coco 8, 9, 10, 14
Chelsea boot 16
Christo 18
Clark, Ossie 19, 26, 27
cloche 17, 30
CND (Campaign for Nuclear Disarmament) 5
Comme des Garçons 30
Concorde 13, 31
consumerism 5, 26, 30
contraceptive *see* Pill
Corfam 16, 29
cotton 25, 26
Courrèges, André 12, 14, 15, 16, 30
couturier 30

dandy 22, 30
de la Renta, Oscar 30
demo 4, 5, 21, 24

denier 28, 30
disposable clothes 29, 30
djellaba 27
dolly-bird look 17, 30
drainpipe trousers 6
Du Pont 28, 29
Dylan, Bob 8, 31

false eyelashes 17
feminism 21
flower power 11, 24
folkie 6, 24, 30
free love 15

Gagarin, Yuri 12, 31
Gap 30
Gee, Cecil 13, 19
Gernreich, Rudi 30
Ginger Group 14, 30
see also Quant, Mary
gloves 17
go-go boot 16
goggles 12
Granny Takes a Trip 11

hairstyle 8, 9, 17, 25, 26, 27, 30
Halston 9
Hare Krishnas 27
hat 8, 9, 12, 16, 17
haute couture 30
Hechter, Daniel 29, 30
hedonism 24, 30
Hell's Angels 25
hippie 5, 11, 15, 17, 20, 24, 25, 26, 27
Hulanicki, Barbara 10

jacket 6, 7, 9, 11, 13
Jagger, Mick 21, 22
jazz 6, 30
jeans 7, 19, 23, 25
'Jesus' sandal 17
jewellery 8, 10, 11, 27

kaftan 23, 26, 27, 30
Kennedy, Jackie 8, 9, 30
Kennedy, John F 8, 31

leather 7, 13, 16, 21, 29
leg make-up 17
LSD 25, 30
Lurex 12, 28
Lycra 29

magazine 20, 21
make-up 17, 20, 25
maxi-skirt 15, 30
metal 13, 29
midi-skirt 15, 30
mini (car) 21
minidress 12, 14, 15
miniskirt 11, 14, 15, 20, 30
mod 6, 7, 22, 29
Mondrian, Piet 19, 30
Muir, Jean 30

nylon 14, 28, 29, 30

op art 10, 18, 30

paisley 14, 22
paper 13, 29
parka 7
Pill 5, 15, 21
pill-box hat 8, 9, 17, 30
pinafore dress 14
plastic 12, 13, 29, 30
platform shoe 17
polo shirt 6
polyester 28, 29
pop art 5, 18
psychedelia 11, 17, 22, 23, 24, 25, 30
PVC 12, 21, 28, 29, 30

Quadrophenia 7
Quant, Mary 5, 9, 10, 14, 16, 28, 29, 30

Rabanne, Paco 13, 29, 30
rayon 28, 30
Rhodes, Zandra 30
Riley, Bridget 18, 31
rockabilly 6
rocker 6, 7

Saint Laurent, Yves 19, 30
Sassoon, Vidal 9, 30
scarf 27
scooter 6
second-hand shop 11
shawl 25
shirt 19, 23, 25
shoe 6, 8, 16, 17, 25
Shrimpton, Jean 20, 21
silk 26, 27, 30
ski pants 7
skirt 9, 14, 15, 16, 25
Small Faces 7
Smith, Mimi 18
space-age 11, 12, 13, 16, 28, 29
Star Trek 12
suede 6, 16
suit 6, 7, 8, 9, 12, 22, 23
'Summer of Love' 25
sunglasses 17
surfer 6, 24

teddy boy 6
tee shirt 11, 19
television 5, 12, 20, 21
tie-dye 11, 19, 30
tights 14, 16, 17, 28
ton-up boy 6
trousers 13, 21, 22, 25, 30
tunic 13, 25
turtleneck sweater 6
Twiggy 20
twin set 7

unisex 26, 27, 30

Valentino 30
velvet 19, 23, 25
Vietnam War 5, 31
vinyl 13, 16, 30
Vogue 10, 18

waistcoat 25
Warhol, Andy 5, 31
winkle-pickers 7, 16, 30
Woodstock 5, 25, 31
wool 26, 30